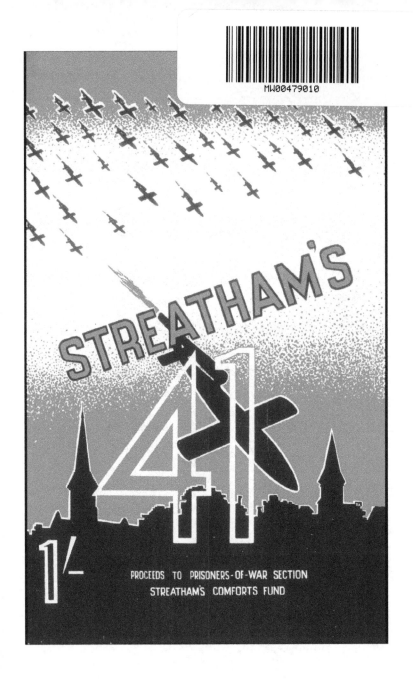

STREATHAM'S

41

1/-

PROCEEDS TO PRISONERS-OF-WAR SECTION
STREATHAM'S COMFORTS FUND

The Naval & Military Press Ltd

Published by

The Naval & Military Press Ltd

Unit 5 Riverside, Brambleside
Bellbrook Industrial Estate
Uckfield, East Sussex
TN22 1QQ England

Tel: +44 (0)1825 749494

www.naval-military-press.com
www.nmarchive.com

*A*S *a tribute*
to the local

CIVIL DEFENCE SERVICES

which came through their
testing time so splendidly,
the cost of producing this book
has been met by

South London Motors, Ltd.,

512/522, Streatham High Road, S.W.16.

————o O o————

THE ENTIRE PROCEEDS GO TO PROVIDE
PARCELS FOR LOCAL PRISONERS.OF.WAR.

First published March, 1945.
Second Edition, April, 1945.

Photographs—see foot of page 47.

FOREWORD

by

SIR ERNEST GOWERS, K.C.B., K.B.E.

(*Senior Regional Commissioner for London*).

I am honoured by the invitation to write a foreword to this publication. I am the more pleased to do so because I have felt an affectionate affinity with the Civil Defence Services of Streatham ever since that Sunday two years ago when, through the kindness of Mr. de Berry, I had the privilege of taking part in a special Civil Defence service at Immanuel Church. There are certain unforgettable things that will always stand out in sharp relief among the jumble of memories that I shall carry away with me from my six years as Regional Commissioner. That Sunday morning is one of them.

" *Damage and casualties have been reported, some of them fatal*." I have often thought, on hearing this bald announcement, that those to whom it meant the loss of their homes and belongings, and perhaps of those dearest to them, deserved to have their sacrifices more worthily and intimately recorded. It was a happy idea to do this for the people of Streatham. It is no longer a secret that they were called on to bear an exceptionally heavy share of that ordeal in which the indomitable fortitude of the sorely-tried Londoner contributed to the glorious issue of the Second Battle of France.

The Prime Minister once advised us to be " *grim and gay*." He also exhorted us, in the same dark days, so to bear ourselves that if the British Empire and its Commonwealth lasted a thousand years, men might still say: " *This was their finest hour*." Here we can learn how thoroughly the people of Streatham took these injunctions to heart, and how unfaltering were their Civil Defence Services in mitigating their sufferings. Those who come after them must not forget it, and I hope that this record will still be read when the events of last summer have become a story of

> *old unhappy far-off things,*
> *and battles long ago.*

Ernest Gowers

STREATHAM

*Map prepared by
Post Warden
Savoie K—93.*

● — **WHERE THEY FELL**

Blast damage was also suffered
from many "near misses," just
over the Boundary.

AN ENLARGEMENT

of this map is obtainable
from :— Divisional Office,
384, Streatham High Road,
S.W.16, price one penny.

4

"STREATHAM'S 41."
A Few Words from the S.D.W.

THE author of this story —or compiler, as he prefers to put it—insists upon remaining anonymous, which is a pity. It can have been no easy work to write up 41 bomb stories, make them all different and maintain (as it appears to me he does) a high level of interest throughout. I, at least, am very grateful to him for all his trouble, and also to Sir Ernest Gowers for contributing a foreword and to Mr. Raymond P. Petty, Chairman of South London Motors Ltd., who has made it financially possible to publish this story.

First, perhaps I ought to make it clear that this is not an official publication, although relaxation of the censorship has permitted facts and figures to be quoted. Part of the story has already appeared in *The Streatham News* and the Editor's permission to reprint is acknowledged with thanks.

It is hoped that nothing is included which can hurt or give offence, but there may well be some heart-burning over what has been left out. " Why isn't the splendid first-aid of Smith mentioned ? " ". . . or the hazardous rescue by Brown ? " " They haven't said much about our service," and so on. Pity the poor scribe—so many things happen simultaneously at any incident so much good work is done by so many persons, that it would take a corps of reporters and reams of paper to cover only one completely.

I propose to seize the opportunity to adjust one over-sight, however, and place on record my deep sense of gratitude to the Divisional Office staff. Not only did they successfully contend with a greatly multiplied volume and variety of work and problems, both routine and operational, but the two Streatham mobile canteens were maintained, staffed and supplied by them throughout the period, and turned out promptly at all hours of the day and night.

There are many well-merited tributes to various services included, all of which I should like to endorse, but primarily the story is told from the warden's view-point, which is only natural as the author is a warden. Let me, therefore, add that in my opinion every branch of Civil Defence performed its own allotted function well, but it was the universal spirit of co-operation, real team-work at all levels, which above any other factor gave Streatham during the flying bomb attacks a standard of service second to none.

Finally, I am surely speaking for every Officer of the Streatham Services, when I say that the real credit for whatever was achieved belongs to the rank and file—they are fine bodies of men and women with whom it is a proud privilege to be associated.

Kenneth Bryant,

SENIOR DISTRICT WARDEN
384, Streatham High Road, London, S.W.16.

STREATHAM'S FIRST : A policeman guards the collected pieces of the fly bomb which hit the old Empire Cinema. (Bomb I.)

BOMB I

RUMOUR had been busy for a day or two regarding an alleged pilotless aircraft which had fallen in East London, when just before 2 a.m. the now only too well-known sound of a flying bomb was heard approaching Streatham.

It dived right into the old Empire cinema and a sheet of flame shot skywards as debris, glass and tiles crashed all around. The cinema was in use as an emergency food store, stacked high with tons and tons of tea, sugar and tinned foodstuffs of all kinds.

Fire broke out, and as Column Officer Williams put it, the heart of the store was "going nicely" by the time the N.F.S. got there. It was a tricky fire to fight, for it was deep-seated and the firemen had to clamber up tottering mountains of tins and packing-cases, with a very real danger of collapse into the fire. The smoke, too, made movement risky. Wardens were to be seen up aloft holding the hose or shining torches to guide footsteps through the smoke.

Total casualties were few, but mention must be made of the rescue of the caretaker of the store by a member of the Light Rescue Party who lived nearby, assisted by a Fire Guard. This caretaker was inside when the bomb fell, but escaped with shock and minor injuries, thanks to this prompt action. An elderly man, he was quickly taken to the First Aid Post at the Baths, but in spite of the severe shaking and his wounds, would not rest until he had telephoned a report to his senior officer in the Ministry of Food.

One of the nearby residents, who was in bed at the time, tells how hardly had the glass finished falling, when he heard a warden climbing the stairs calling out, " Stay where you are, I'm coming." Very glad he was to have followed this advice, for by the warden's torch was revealed a floor littered with broken glass—very menacing to bare feet.

Although this was mainly an " N.F.S." incident, the Streatham Welfare Scheme (a joint organisation of wardens and W.V.S.) operating at its first fly bomb incident, dealt excellently with over 120 persons requiring temporary shelter.

The neighbouring railway line was blocked by debris, but soon after dawn this was cleared and trains ran normally. It was interesting to see lineswomen hard at it repairing the telephone lines, climbing the posts with quite professional skill.

It is worthy of record that the Post Warden of J90 put two wardens in charge who had only just completed their training as Incident Officers, and they came through very well.

The S.D.W. was seen carrying what looked like a piece of battered and perforated corrugated iron, but it proved to be part of the bomb complete with German lettering. This was hustled to headquarters by car and hustled back again a few hours later when the R.A.F. intelligence staff arrived in search of all possible clues, for little detail was known of these bombs at that time.

To save space the following abbreviations of Wardens' rank are used throughout :—

S.D.W.	Senior District Warden
D.W.	District Warden
D.D.W.	Deputy District Warden
D.W.W.	District Welfare Warden
P.W.	Post Warden
D.P.W.	Deputy Post Warden
P.W.W.	Post Welfare Warden
S.W.	Senior Warden
I.O.	Incident Officer

The Chief Warden inspected the scene early next day and Admiral Sir Edward Evans, one of London's Regional Commissioners, visited the incident about noon, accompanied by the Borough Controller, and was extremely interested in all he saw.

Full credit must be given to the N.F.S. and their salvage section, for by far the greater part of the food was saved and transported under M.O.F. supervision to other depots. Several wardens from various posts rallied round to an emergency call in the afternoon and helped form the human chain which loaded the lorries.

The shop of a Dyer and Cleaner was completely wrecked by blast, yet not a single garment was destroyed. They all required recleaning, of course, but the proprietor regarded that as a detail, compared with the possibility of having to hand back :—

" *One blasted lady's costume.*"
" *One, ditto, gent's plus fours.*"

At the request of the police, the Home Guard took over the task of protecting the many damaged shops. They set about this in a thorough manner by throwing a line of men across the width of the High Road and advancing with rifles at the ready, challenging everybody. This had the effect of removing from the scene all unnecessary sightseers, and potential looters (if any). By mischance, some members of the Fire Guard were also eliminated (not liquidated) by this military manoeuvre, but that was "just one of those things." This guarding of damaged property is a rather dull and boring job for those doing it, but very much appreciated by the property owners, and the Home Guard helped the police frequently in this way.

One of the buildings severely damaged and rendered unusable was the Methodist Church, in which there was scheduled to take place on the following day, a Civic Service in connection with the Religion and Life Week, to be attended by His Worship the Mayor of Wandsworth. The service was transferred to St. Leonard's Church and duly held. The large congregation remained steady as a rock, whilst a flying bomb vibrated the very air as it passed right overhead to crash well within earshot, just over the boundary of a neighbouring division of the borough.

A side-light of the flying bomb attacks was that they completely wrecked the follow-up work of the combined churches, which was proposed to take place subsequent to this Week, but the clergy found ample opportunity to contact the man and woman in-the-street—(the term is only too apt, sometimes they had nowhere else to be), and many of them rose to the occasion magnificently. During a particularly " busy " spell, somebody said it seemed that the " Religion and Life " Campaign had been followed by a period of " Devilry and Death."

BOMBS 2, 3 & 4 About 48 hours after the first, Streatham's fly bomb No. 2 crashed in Pathfield Road (Post J.87). Fifteen minutes later No. 3 fell in Penrith Street (Post I.78) and to complete the picture Downton Avenue (Post K.97) had No. 4 only ten minutes after that. Here, indeed, was a situation to test Civil Defence to the limit, for the bombs had all fallen on residential areas and the blast damage was enormous ; only comparable in previous experience with that caused by the land-mine which fell in the Vale during the 1940-41 blitz.

The number of houses reported damaged by these three flying bombs was just under 3,000. That Saturday night was pitch-dark and further bombs continued to roar over to the accompaniment of a terrific barrage from the ack-ack guns, and it was in these circumstances that Streatham's Civil Defence tackled their new problems. As is well-known now, the ratio of casualties to material damage proved to be miraculously small, but this was not known at the time and, until the house-to-house check-up had been completed, it was impossible for the respective Incident Officers to assess accurately just how much trouble they had to handle—but they did know it was plenty. Similarly, the Party Leaders, learning the widespread nature of the damage, prudently assumed that they would require considerable reinforcements.

All this meant that lines of communication were crowded with urgent calls, and the Streatham telephone exchange certainly put up a grand show that night under very trying conditions. Divisional Office, for instance, had over 100 calls, and Borough Sub-Control, as the operational focus for two divisions must have had several times that number.

One important factor which emerged, and deserves full recognition, for it was common to all fly bomb incidents, was that the extent of damage inevitably involved the houses and homes of the very wardens who handled the incident. Time and time again, wardens reported for duty, having struggled out of a window or through a back garden because it was the only way of getting out from a wrecked home. Frequently this involved leaving in trying circumstances (to put it mildly) a wife, aged parents or even children, but never once did the wardens in any area fail to rise to the occasion, putting the needs of others before their own misfortunes.

Here, perhaps, it is opportune to record the outstanding success of the automatic reinforcement scheme '' laid-on '' by the District Wardens a few weeks before the attacks commenced. Many an I.O., short of personnel for the dozens of jobs he had to fill, had cause to thank the foresight shown and the generous way in which all posts operated the scheme to help their stricken neighbours.

Space will not permit detailed accounts of any incident, even if all the material was available, but here are some of the facts of these three :—

J.87. D.P.W. Harrison acted as I.O., being " backed-up " by the Post Warden and two Deputy District Wardens. The casualties were about 40, including 2 fatal. The care of the homeless was in the excellent hands of D.W.W. Faulkner. Many of them were temporarily sheltered in the trenches on the Common and it proved possible to send a Y.M.C.A. canteen there to provide tea before they made the journey to the Rest Centre or other accommodation. Heavy Rescue Party Leader Slater took abnormal risks in the operation, by working for some time in a position overhung by a very dangerous wall and displayed a quality of leadership worthy of high praise.

Mrs. Sheppard, a member of the W.V.S. and wife of the Deputy District Warden, did good work by taking hot drinks to the working parties, notwithstanding the fact that her house was badly damaged. The rather long gap before the arrival of the mobile canteen which occurred on this occasion made her efforts doubly welcome. It is said that the Borough Controller, who visited the incidents during the night, himself went seeking the keyholder of the stores, whose safety measures were so good that the mobile canteens could get no supplies. Needless to say, no hold-up occurred subsequently.

The operations were pressed forward with vigour and, having regard to the wide devastation and many new factors it introduced, all services emerged with credit.

I.78. This fly bomb was almost certainly the most damaging of Streatham's 41, for it affected no less than 1,671 houses. The I.O. was D.P.W. Long, who had only completed his course and exam. three days before, but handled a trying task very well indeed. He received full backing from Mr. Waight, then " Acting " I District Warden, who was on the scene very quickly, also from the Post Warden and, indeed, all wardens of I.78 and other posts, who rallied round.

A particularly striking feature was that warden " first-aiders " dealt with 150 slightly injured persons in the adjoining Rest Centre. Miss Windridge was one of these wardens and received congratulations from a doctor for the standard of her work. Known affectionately as " Windy "—a most inappropriate nickname—she was to be seen at most I District incidents with her first-aid kit.

Whilst one is reluctant to mention individuals when all did so well, yet warden Bell is surely an exceptional case, for although he received a fractured arm and face wounds from his dented helmet, he assisted in rescue work and other duties until forced to go to hospital the following day. Warden Johnson was only slightly less commendable, carrying on despite severe blasting.

Photo : Streatham News.

" THEY ALSO SERVE— " : Following the close of an incident, a contact warden stands by
on the scene to direct enquirers and post-raid services. (Bomb 2.)

A contingent of Tooting Home Guard (the whole of 1 District is in their area) gave valuable aid on Sunday morning in debris clearance and the continuing search for missing persons.

K.97. The point made earlier regarding the damage to the homes of the " resident " wardens who handle the incidents and the trying conditions under which they go into action was forcibly illustrated here. An action station received a direct hit and warden Gladwin, who had returned there after reporting at the post, was killed outright, together with his wife—a Fire Guard Street Party Leader. The Post Welfare Warden was incapacitated, and the Post Warden's home wrecked, together with those of other wardens living in that sector. Notwithstanding this, and the newness of the problems created by fly bombs, it was not long before D.P.W. Neal had taken over as I.O. and established effective control. The services arrived quickly and some very fine rescue work was carried out, of which more may be heard later. The K District Warden and his deputies gave consistant support to the I.O. throughout the night.

Mrs. Begg, a lady warden, was particularly commended by the Heavy Rescue Party for the cool and efficient way she carried out the tricky job of " Occupants' Checker "—her home, too, had been blasted.

Again there were plenty of homeless to be cared for, and D.W.W. Belham soon arrived and took over this work. Many were directed to a nearby hall, and from there removed

11

to a Rest Centre by Green Line coaches. This was no pleasure trip with further fly bombs sailing overhead and incessant gunfire. L.A.C. Marks (ex Divisional Office) who was on leave, spent it helping, and amongst other jobs, rode on the bonnet of a coach to direct the driver.

It was 10 p.m. Sunday before this incident was closed, a long delay being caused by trying to find two persons who had gone away but not advised the wardens.

The three big incidents happening almost simultaneously, created in Streatham at one fell swoop, post-raid problems of a variety and magnitude only reached gradually elsewhere. The W.V.S. had opened up three Incident Inquiry Points adjacent to the bombed areas and they were besieged with inquiries of all kinds. Here let it be said that these I.I.Ps. were a real godsend at every incident, and no praise can be too high for the W.V.S. personnel that manned them. There seemed to be an inexhaustible supply of tactful sympathy, practical advice and concrete assistance. It is impossible to name even a fraction of these helpers, but it would certainly be their wish that tribute should be paid to the leaders—Mrs. Crisp, Mrs. Cronk (until both injured) Mrs. Knight, Mrs. Larlham, Mrs. Bailey, Mrs. Irwin, Mrs. Kinnersley and Mrs. Skinner.

Shortly before mid-day on Sunday an appeal came for emergency feeding, since in many houses cooking facilities no longer existed. A 'phone call from C.D. Divisional Office to the duty officer at County Hall quickly led to the L.C.C. Meals Service undertaking to open up Madeira Hall and supply a meal during the afternoon—this notwithstanding the fact this building had itself been severely damaged by the first fly bomb. Inspector Pateman then arranged for a police loudspeaker car to tour the area making the announcement. Just another instance of the universal spirit of co-operation and desire to get things done— to give practical help quickly.

By Monday morning it was apparent that a major hardship was the amount of travelling involved for the bombed-out to contact the many Post Raid services. One was here, another there, and the third, fourth and fifth in still different places. Moreover, nobody seemed too sure where they were, anyway, and a terrible lot of wrong information was being given, which led to many fruitless journeys.

For example, the nearest office of the Assistance Board was at East Hill, Wandsworth, a long and awkward journey, well-nigh impossible for a mother with young children, especially during the frequent "Alerts." Mr. Hart, the Board's Senior Area Officer, however, immediately assented to the Senior District Warden's urge that a different arrangement should be made, and that

Photo : Streatham News.

THE FIRST V.I IN THE VALE : Falling within a stone's throw of where a land mine fell in 1941, this fly bomb wrecked hundreds of homes. Note the undamaged mirror on the bedroom wall. (Bomb 6.)

afternoon they saw Canon Salmon, who readily let the Board have St. Leonard's Hall. A uniformed mobile team of the Board, thoroughly experienced in dealing with special situations and under the able leadership of Mr. Balden (Area Officer) was summoned from Birmingham and opened up at 9.30 next morning. Nice work. They quickly won a reputation for prompt and efficient service. Mr. Ladell, the recently retired Streatham station-master, acted as honorary receptionist, thus releasing a skilled man for the counter. Canon Salmon took a close interest in this work and, after waging a stern battle with various authorities, arranged that the Salvation Army should provide free tea and biscuits to all waiting applicants—a much appreciated gesture of practical sympathy.

To check the mis-direction, a sheet of detailed information was quickly prepared at the Civil Defence Divisional Office and widely circulated. It was so useful that two revised versions were issued, pending the opening of the central Information Centre much later.

The next damage was when Post J.85 got the blast from a very near-miss, which landed just over the Croydon (Norbury) boundary. Over 500 Streatham houses were damaged and the casualties included five wardens—fortunately none serious.

BOMB 5 Two days later K.92 got their first flying bomb, and it made the usual nasty mess of the surrounding buildings. The I.O. was S.W. Morley, another candidate at the exam. a few days before, and he discharged the responsibility very well. A remarkable escape was that of a man inside a sand-bag enclosure only a few yards from the bomb when it exploded.

The N.F.S. arrived at this incident in force, although there was no fire, under an arrangement which worked to the great advantage of Civil Defence throughout the attacks. This co-operation of the N.F.S. at non-fire incidents was probably the biggest single factor in the new methods employed. From the top of high towers at the fire stations, constant watch was maintained (not a pleasant job) and immediately a fly bomb was seen to fall in the district, at least five appliances and crews moved off at speed, invariably arriving at the incident within a matter of minutes. In the day-time, when nearly all the part-time wardens were out of the area at work, this arrangement alone made it practical to deal adequately with the damage situation. Tribute must be paid to the way in which the N.F.S. quickly learnt C.D. procedure, recognised the authority of the Incident Officer and willingly worked under the skilled direction of the Heavy Rescue Party. Column Officer Williams and Company Officer Langford were to be seen everywhere ; as, indeed, was Divisional Officer Baker, although Streatham is only a small part of his Fire area.

BOMB 6 The same day, in the evening, Streatham Vale (Post J.84) had their first fly bomb, which exploded in a culvert which runs between the back gardens of two roads. Three roads were drastically affected, and there were over 40 casualties. Warden Keightley, L.A.R.P. (well-known as a C.D. lecturer), acted as I.O., most ably assisted by warden Watts, who ran out of his chemist's shop to help. At that time in the evening large numbers of residents were returning from business and there were tragic home-comings for many.

Any number of volunteer helpers set to work feverishly on rescue operations, services flooded in from Streatham and other Wandsworth Divisions, also from Mitcham and Croydon. The local Fire Guard were especially good, and many Home Guard helped too.

With so much going on at the came time, and casualties being sent away from several points, it was no light task to keep track of them. Warden Pressdee as Loading Ground Warden tackled this job very efficiently. The many other functions performed by wardens were also well done.

The mobile canteen presented to Civil Defence by the residents and traders of Streatham was early on the scene, manned by Divisional Office staff, and proved a wonderful boon, as it did over and over again.

There were quite a number of homeless to be sheltered. Some went to Eardley Road and Defoe Road Rest Centres, many were housed locally by friends, others were transferred by V.C.P. cars to more remote addresses. All this was fixed up by the Streatham Welfare Scheme. The warden side of this Organisation was represented by D.W.W. Faulkner and P.W.W. Lawrence, and the W.V.S. by Mrs. Bailey, Mrs. Thompson and many others. Mrs. Nutting, Borough Organiser, also managed to get over from Wandsworth. The V.C.P. cars were of immense assistance throughout the bombing in helping to get away old folks, invalids and others not able to use public transport. Mileage had to be watched carefully and on this occasion when a lady warden came into the Incident Inquiry Point saying she had two expectant mothers to be moved, the usual question was put " How far have they to go ? " The reply, however, was unexpected—" Well, one of them, 5 weeks."

As one would expect in the Vale, good neighbourliness and self-help were to be seen everywhere. P.W. Thompson ably organised the removal of furniture from damaged houses and with the help of local firms' lorries and vans plus those sent in by the Borough, this aspect of the job was completed by Sunday. The N.F.S. also gave great help in the post-raid clear-up both here and at many other incidents. It also marked the first

appearance in Streatham of a Ministry of Works flying squad of workmen to tackle first-aid repairs.

Another novelty was the attendance at mid-day Friday of a mobile bath unit consisting of hot shower-bath cubicles complete with towels and soap. The bathrooms of many houses had been rendered useless, so that the opportunity to get rid of the ingrained dust and grime was most welcome.

BOMB 7 Streatham was to get no respite and just before seven next morning a fly bomb crashed in Barrow Road. Pathfield, Lewin, Natal and surrounding roads were also badly blasted, many houses suffering damage for the second time in a week.

The heart of the incident consisted of four completely collapsed large houses. Each presented a long job for the Rescue Services and the immediate problem was to decide where to work first—where were the trapped casualties ?

The wardens gave the picture according to their Occupants Cards (very recently checked) and neighbours helped, but nevertheless for $2\frac{1}{2}$ hours one of the Rescue parties aided by wardens, N.F.S., Home Guard and other volunteers, worked desperately shifting tons of debris, only to learn that the supposed casualty had been traced by the police to a South Coast town. Is it any wonder Civil Defence would like it made compulsory to notify wardens of removals ?

BLASTED. Damage at the top of Amesbury Avenue. The bomb fell on houses the other side of the road (Bomb 12.)

sequences for casualty and rescuer. Once the casualty is reached, a doctor takes over direction and the release is carried out according to the condition of the victim. Doctor Lawson was present on this occasion.

This rescue was typical of the fine work performed during the fly bomb attacks. Within little more than an hour, verbal contact had been made by tunnelling in towards the trapped casualty, who was a 17-year-old girl. Oxygen was administered by tube and the Heavy Rescue Officers kept up a running conversation with her

Whilst the Light and Heavy Rescue Leaders were completing their reconnaissance, a lady Fire Guard heard a faint cry in a certain part of the debris. Quickly this was confirmed and the plan of rescue laid down by the Heavy Rescue Leader. Many Streatham trapped casualties owe their very lives to this skilled planning by L.C.C. Station Officers Pavey and Strudwick or their deputies Elliott and Regan and the way in which the Rescue parties executed their plans. Speed in rescue is essential, but so, too, is a sound method of approach, or further collapse may well occur, with fatal con-

throughout the four hours the rescue took. The casualty showed great spirit and when one arm was freed, asked for and received a wet flannel to wash her face. On learning the time, she jokingly said, '' Oh dear, I shall be late—missed the workman's fare too. Never mind, I'll get the cheap mid-day rate on the trams.'' No, not rambling nor hysteria, just plain British pluck.

D.P.W. Harrison, of J.87, again acted as I.O. and was warmly commended by his senior officers. The backing he received from wardens of J.87, 86 and other posts was admirable. A.T.S. personnel voluntarily gave assistance shifting debris. The Vicar of Immanuel Church and his curate were untiring in their efforts to assist the aged and homeless, whilst the Welfare Organisation was again right in the picture and, of course, the W.V.S. Incident Inquiry Point.

During the afternoon Col. Llewellin, the Minister of Food, visited the scene and, amongst other points, was anxious to learn if the mobile canteens were giving satisfactory service.

BOMB Soon after midnight
8 K.97 took its second fly bomb—a direct hit on a modern block of flats in Streatham Hill. The building stood it well and there was no collapse, hence few serious casualties. The contrast with the Downton Avenue incident was so striking that a second search was made in case any casualties had been overlooked. Whilst the N.F.S. were helping the wardens with this task, a lady rushed up to one of them, crying " My husband ! Oh, my husband ! ! '' Said the gallant fireman, '' That'll be all right, madam—just tell us where he is and we'll get him out in no time.'' '' He's up in the West End on fire watch,'' came the surprising answer.

Streatham Hill Theatre was placed at the disposal of the I.O. (Warden Steel) and provided an excellent medical aid post, with plenty of light, comfort, hot water and even tea. Doctors Bailey and Melvin were present on this and many other incidents.

A most acceptable form of help was provided by a military unit, who sent a bulldozer, which made short work of clearing the debris from the main road, thus aiding both the removal of casualties by ambulance and the police in restoring normal traffic, and at that time Streatham Hill was was a vital through route for Second Front supplies.

By 5 a.m. it was possible to close this incident. A nice quick job—very well done. This includes the welfare work of Mr. Belham and the Incident Inquiry Point run by the W.V.S. under Mrs. Skinner.

BOMB The next incident
9 was a day-time one— the fly bomb falling in Thrale Road (Post Area I.81) about four o'clock. The services, including N.F.S., police and warden reinforcements from many posts, arrived promptly. The damage was extensive, 1,000 houses being affected. Casualties numbered over 30, including a lad who was pushing a handcart within 25 yards of where the bomb fell. The cart was blown to fragments, but the lad was alive and after attention from a doctor was rushed by ambulance to hospital. There skilled surgeons and devoted nurses successfully fought for his life, and although still in an evacuation hospital, he is going on well.

Several houses occupied by local doctors were affected. That of Dr. Morrish caught fire, but this was quickly brought under control by the N.F.S. A large tree had been blown down, blocking Fayland Avenue and heavy rain set in which made everything more difficult for the services and multiplied the hardship of those whose roofs had been lifted by the blast.

D.D.W. Ames acted as I.O., with Miss Rippon as clerk. Lady wardens were naturally predominant (the men being mostly out of the area at work) and included Mrs. Goldsworthy and Mrs. Wagstaff (who did a splendid job of first aid) Mrs. Braham, Mrs. B. K. Smith and Miss Milnes, I District Welfare Warden. Head Fire Guard Turner and Senior Fire Guard Sainsbury gave valuable assistance, as indeed they did at every I District incident, and some of the others too.

One especially paltry thing happened on this occasion. A casualty about to be removed to hospital was worried about the care of her dog. A woman standing by offered to look after it, but neither she nor the dog have been seen since, and the owner on her recovery seemed more distressed by this than the loss of her home.

The funeral of warden Gladwin and his wife, who had been killed by the Downton Avenue bomb, took place at St. Margaret's Church on Monday afternoon and was attended by many of his fellow wardens from K.97, led by Post Warden Lumley. The Senior District Warden, the Divisional Officer and Divisional Fire Guard were also present and several members of the W.V.S. Just as the service ended and the bearers rose to carry the coffins from the church, the rasping note of an approaching fly bomb was heard. The mourners remained quietly standing without a waver as the bomb roared overhead, to explode a mile or two further on. It was an impressive and tense moment which few present will ever forget.

BOMB 10 Poor old K.97 took its third knock within ten days, when the next fly bomb crashed in Barcombe Avenue, Streatham Hill—a direct hit on No. 24. Again there was widespread devastation and many found the first-aid repairs they had effected were " gone with the wind." Warden Steele (who was for a period Post Warden of K.97) took charge as I.O. and was ably backed by the other wardens, including D.W. Garrett, with his deputies, T. J. Bryant and C. T. Hack. P.W. Lumley concentrated on the lines of communication — a vital but non-spectacular side of incident procedure.

Another excellent repeat performance was given by Mrs. Begg as occupants checker, ably assisted by other wardens—there was no delay in supplying the Rescue leaders with full and accurate information where to work.

Dr. Bailey and Dr. Margaret Melvin rendered excellent service, as they did at the previous two K.97 incidents (and many others). Dr. Sinclair did a specially good job in climbing high into a dangerous structure to attend to a critically injured casualty before removal.

Although the bomb fell after 1 a.m., the Locarno Dance Hall was immediately opened by Messrs. Chaperlin & Davis, as a temporary haven for the homeless and casualties. Over 1,000 cups of tea were supplied during the night to those unfortunate people, also to the services and nearby shelterers. D.W.W. Belham and P.W.W. Alexander collected the homeless and when daylight came, they were transported to Rest Centres, having been very comfortably accommodated in the meantime, thanks to the Locarno.

As at most incidents, dozens of people should be mentioned —but the services rather expect to be taken for granted. Some of the others who helped were : a member of the American Red Cross (Mr. Freebury) who assisted at all three incidents, and shortly afterwards left for Normandy. A nurse who carried a child all the way from Barcombe Avenue to the first aid post at Brixton Hill— then walked back to minister to the minor casualties gathered in Locarno. A member of the N.F.S. (Tolley ?) who bent his back under a broken waterpipe to protect a trapped casualty, and although soaked to the skin, stuck it until the water could be turned off. Pte. Anderson of the Streatham Home Guard who was outstandingly helpful on all these occasions.

BOMB Just after 8 o'clock
II next morning K.92 had its second fly bomb, which fell in the gardens between Valley and Harborough Roads, wrecking Sunnyhill Rd. School, which has been closed ever since. It was providential that the children had not arrived. P.W. Brimicombe took charge, and with the help of wardens who willingly postponed their departure to business, soon established control. The bomb falling on soft ground, there was a sizeable crater and some very interesting bits were found in it, all of which were taken over by the police. The services rendered by the police are rather apt to be overlooked, but it would be a grave injustice not to record the admirable way they carried out their own duties and co-operated to the full with Civil Defence throughout the fly bomb attacks—always willing to help, but carefully refraining from interference. Names of senior officers of the Streatham police who were on many of the incidents are Sub-Divisional Inspector Pateman, Inspectors Candler, Sheath and Traylor. The first named was subsequently awarded the King's Police Medal.

There were no fatal casualties and only four to hospital, but two of the wardens, Mr. and Mrs. Kidby, were injured. The sixty homeless were well cared for by P.W.W. Masters and Miss Pollock. The assistant Chief Warden (Mr. H. W. Fray) visited this incident, amongst others.

The United Dairies bottling depot was not seriously affected, although it received some damage on this and other occasions. At a later date the Minister of Food paid the depot a visit and congratulated all concerned on the maintenance of milk distribution throughout the trying period.

BOMB 12 Before mid-day yet another fly bomb crashed on the Streatham Hill district, this time at the top of Amesbury Avenue in the area of Post K.98. Police, N.F.S., Heavy and Light Rescue parties, ambulances and doctors were quickly on the scene. Naturally, there were few K.98 wardens available at that time of the day, but willing reinforcements rushed in from surrounding posts. Actually the first I.O. (Warden Ward) was from K.97 and he carried on until S.W. Sudell of K.98 arrived. P.W. Gorringe of K.96 took charge at the K.98 post; whilst others present were the Senior District Warden, D.D.W. T. J. Bryant, Canon Salmon, head of the Welfare Organisation and D.W.W. Faulkner of J, who functioned for Mr. Belham until P.W.W. Hunt took over.

D.P.W. Barker returned hurriedly from business and exercised general supervision. P.W. Sumner had received a nasty eye injury from glass, but insisted on remaining at the incident until ordered to hospital by the Senior District Warden. It was weeks before he could return to duty and then unfortunately minus an eye.

Thanks to the smart work of the parties, plus the accuracy of the occupants check carried out by wardens Bayliff and Riches (the census cards proving most useful), the operation quickly resolved itself into a search for the wife of a Dutchman and their " three lovely children," as the neighbours described them. Alas, when found they were all four beyond human aid. Yet another tragic " triumph " for the indiscriminate warfare practised by the German master-race.

BOMB 13 The third fly bomb to fall in Streatham within the 12 hours crashed in the Vale at the apex of Sherwood Avenue and Glenister Park Road, almost on top of Post J.83.

P.W. Joslin immediately took charge as I.O. The turn-out of services was particularly brisk, the N.F.S. being present in very large numbers, also the Home Guard and both assisted with the rescue work. The Home Guard flung out such an effective cordon round the incident that even the S.D.W. couldn't get his car through, however, he walked. Although damage was considerable, serious casualties were few, but three wardens were injured. Dr. Sinclair was again prominent, doing good work—so, too, was the Streatham mobile canteen.

BOMB 14 Streatham's fourteenth fly bomb fell mid-morning next day on a house in Hoadley Road,

Photo : *South Thames Press Agency.*

" CAREFUL NOW " : Under the guidance of a doctor, a male casualty is lifted on to a stretcher. The Anderson Shelter was in a ground floor room, but the room and house vanished. (Bomb 13.)

right next to the home of D.W.W. Belham, which was wrecked, but his family were uninjured. D.P.W. Waight was fortunately available to act as I.O. and P.W. Hawes returned from business before operations had been proceeding very long. From the casualty angle this was the ''cheapest'' fly bomb incident to date, only one requiring removal to hospital. It was cleared quickly and well.

Another of the homes destroyed by this bomb was that of Mr. and Mrs. Pitts—the latter so well-known locally as Staff Commandant of the British Red Cross Society and Honorary Secretary of the Penny-a-week Fund. They took their misfortune with typical pluck and good humour.

Mrs. Nutting, Borough Organizer of the W.V.S., immediately offered a room in her nearby home for use as the Incident Inquiry Point and it was gratefully accepted.

BOMB 15 The next day was Saturday, and a fly bomb crashed on the Wandsworth Borough housing estate in Freshwater Road early in the afternoon. Most of the Civil Defence personnel working on this incident must have had a very late dinner that day. Services arrived quickly and in force, especially the N.F.S.

"DAMAGE WAS CAUSED " : Rescuers of many services at the Sherwood Avenue and Glenister Park incident. (Bomb 13.)

The L.A.A.S. practice which had recently been introduced, of attaching an ambulance to the tail of the convoy of the fire appliances meant that it was on the scene early. Some casualties were removed in other vehicles and this caused difficulty later, since no record of the names was kept. It meant sending messengers to all likely hospitals to secure lists of admittances, for no incident is ever closed until every person has been accounted for beyond any shadow of doubt.

D.D.W. Ames was the I.O., with Mrs. B. K. Smith as clerk. D.W. Waight was also prominent, whilst rescue work went forward well under Deputy Station Officer Regan. One of the human chains manhandling skips of debris was composed of members of all the C.D. services, plus representatives of the Army, R.A.F., Home Guard and civilian passers-by on their way home from work. It was typical of the universal desire to help, a grand spirit which did much to lighten the burden of this period.

Mr. David Robertson, M.P. for Streatham, arrived at the incident five minutes after it happened, with the Senior District Warden and Divisional Fire Guard, but left immediately, saying that it was no place for sightseers, who would merely hamper the services.

BOMB 16 About two hours after this bomb fell, when the situation was just about clear, down came another, only 150 yards away, with a roar and crash of collapsing houses. All personnel went flat, whilst the mobile canteen, with staff inside, bounced on its tyres. This was the only occasion that a Streatham post area had two fly bomb incidents in one day, and the wardens of I.79 are to be congratulated on the way they just "moved over" and carried on, with dinner even more remote.

Mr. Waight, the District Warden, and others ran to the scene and set up the Incident Officer's control point before the cloud of smoke and dust from the explosion had settled. Services came quickly and worked with an efficiency increasing with practice.

A slight fire was soon extinguished by the N.F.S. Five wards of a nearby hospital were badly blasted, but the First Aid Post under Dr. Abrahams was able to function despite a severe shake-up.

Later in the incident Divisional Commander Baker sent N.F.S. working parties into the hospital to clear up and repair the black-out, a much-appreciated action. One pathetic sight was to see the efforts being made to salvage the scattered stock of a small shop, whose proprietress was a casualty worrying over her loss.

The total casualties at these two incidents were 66, of which three were fatal, including a passing cyclist in Rectory Lane whose identification was a problem in itself.

Alderman Jordan, Deputy Chief Warden, who was present most of the time, expressed himself well-satisfied, and indeed I.79, assisted by wardens from every other post in I District, came through this double ordeal very well indeed.

BOMB 17 I District was to get a third flying bomb that day and whilst it was still daylight Aldrington Road in I.81 was hit. The most severely damaged house was the home of Mrs. Cronk, a prominent W.V.S. member, and stopping with her for the week-end was Mrs. Crisp, the Streatham Sub-Centre Organiser. Both were seriously injured, but are now well on the way to complete recovery. Mrs. Crisp has since said that although trapped and injured, she was fully conscious all the time, and not for a moment did she doubt that the Civil Defence services would find and rescue her. Fortunately they did, for Mrs. Crisp is of the salt of the earth, and had only stopped in Streatham that night from a sheer sense of duty, for her home is at Wimbledon and her husband had asked her to join him at Cambridge for the weekend.

Mr. Archer, only recently appointed Post Warden of I.81, proved an able I.O., and was well supported by the other wardens.

BOMB 18 After a Sunday free from an incident in Streatham, the attack was resumed before five o'clock one morning, when a fly bomb crashed on the railway embankment immediately behind a row of houses in Besley Street. Prompt steps were taken by the wardens to advise the railway company in case the track had been rendered unsafe.

A Home Guard Officer reported to the I.O. (Warden Usher of Post I.77) within a matter of minutes of the bomb falling, despite the hour. Reinforcements of wardens came from many posts, including J.84, a pleasing instance of inter-district co-operation. Two of the lads who acted as C.D. Messengers (Randall and Letchford) were quickly on the scene from Post I.77.

Parked up among the Fire appliances, thus indicating very early arrival, was the little green van used by J Head Fire Guard Cotton. There can have been few Streatham incidents at which he was not present, ever-willing to lend a hand at anything, from sweeping the road clear of debris upwards.

In addition to the usual services, the Metropolitan Water Board and Gas Repair Party were also present. Although not spectacular, the work done by these and other Utility Companies was essential to the handling of many incidents.

Many of these small terrace houses were occupied by elderly folk, and the spirit they displayed was splendid — well could the I.O. reply to the routine question " Morale ? Excellent.''

A day or so later, the local M.P. (Mr. David Robertson) was visiting the scene, and called at one of the blitzed houses. The husband asked him in and through to the kitchen, where mother was sitting with her legs in a bath of hot water " to get the swelling down a bit.'' She was full of praise for father, who had spent the day cleaning the debris from the loft, without any outside help. Then jointly they drew attention to the grandfather clock, which nearly reached the ceiling, the case of which was studded with fragments of glass which the explosion had driven in. " But it never stopped, sir, not for a minute,'' they exclaimed with pride.

" Why don't you go to the Rest Centre for a spell,'' they were asked. " Well, we did try it, and everybody was most kind—but we are both over seventy and would rather be here in our own home.'' " How do you manage for cooking ? '' " Ah, that is a bit trying, for the gas-stove is in the outhouse, with no roof, windows or door left, and often when I go back the gas has blown out.'' " Have you any family who could help you clear up ? '' " Well, we have some sons and daughters, but they are all married with homes of their own and we haven't told them that we've been bombed, for they would only worry about us, and we can manage all right, thank you.''

How can Hitler hope to break people with a spirit like that ?

There were 27 casualties at this incident, four of which were fatal. The rescue operations were completed in three hours, and permission to close the incident granted by the Controller at 8 a.m.

BOMB 19 Earlier, whilst rescue operations were still proceeding, the C.D. personnel had seen another flying bomb tip in its flight and make its fateful dive on Streatham Hill. Senior officers ran for their cars and hurried away to the new incident. The bomb had struck the side of Streatham Hill Theatre and blown an enormous hole in the brickwork wall. Barrhill Road was covered with the displaced brickwork, quite impassable for vehicles and like a rocky foreshore scramble for those on foot.

The theatre management had permitted members of the staff and their friends to sleep in the underground bars and lounges as a kind of de-luxe shelter. Immediately the N.F.S. and Rescue parties penetrated into this part of the theatre and conducted a thorough search. Some casualties were quickly recovered and despatched to hospital, including Mr. T. J. Bryant, the K Deputy District Warden, also his wife and son, who were sheltering there since their own home had been wrecked in an earlier incident. Later, and after a prolonged search, Mrs. Bryant's mother was recovered, but unfortunately she was dead. Mr. Bryant, who has a splendid record of Civil Defence work equalled by few in Streatham, made a good recovery up to a point, but he was advised to take a prolonged convalescence in the Isle of Wight and was still away six months later.

Warden Ward acted as I.O. on this occasion—the fourth fly bomb to fall in the area of Post K.97, the wardens of which again acquitted themselves very well.

Special praise is due to Senior Fire Guard Eggleton for the way he carried out his duties, notwithstanding the fact that his wife had been taken to hospital seriously injured.

Whilst the theatre incident was at height, I.77 at the other end of Streatham, received considerable damage and a casualty, from one of the many " near-misses " which fell just over the Mitcham boundary.

BOMB 20 No. 3 that day was to fall in Buckleigh Road, and extensive damage was done there, also in Northanger and other adjoining roads. Q.R.C.D. Letts, who works nearby, and like many other part-time wardens was wearing his uniform ready for such emergencies, dashed round on his cycle, first to the incident, then to Post J.87 to get the warden on duty to send in the Express Report. Returning in quick time, he just beat the first two N.F.S. teams, who immediately searched the damaged properties, recovered many of the casualties and despatched them to hospital. Wardens from J.86 had by then arrived and set up incident control, D.P.W. Osborn being in charge. Some very good first aid was carried out by the wardens on this occasion.

The incident followed the normal course and was cleared up in a business-like manner. Twenty-three casualties were

"SHE SHOULD BE HERE " : The search for a trapped casualty goes forward. Note the many N.F.S. The wrecked house on the right was the home of District Welfare Warden Belham. (Bomb 14).

yard-stick by which Civil Defence compared incidents, but it does not do to overlook the enormous amount of suffering inflicted on those who, although uninjured, were rendered completely homeless, or left with no windows, no doors, ceilings down and half a roof. And the weather—it rained ! and rained ! ! and rained ! ! ! multiplying the damage and hardship tenfold.

Amongst the victims in this category on this occasion was P. W. Fraser, whose home was a total loss. Unable to get rehoused locally, he has nevertheless continued to carry out

taken to hospital and six to the First Aid Post.

BOMB 21 This was to prove Streatham's "busiest" day, for the fourth fly bomb (excluding the I.77 near-miss) to fall in the division within a period of 14 hours, chose Kingsmead Road in K.100 as its target. D.P.W. Grose arrived early and took charge, finding the N.F.S. already well down to the job of reconnaissance.

From the casualty angle this was a " cheap " incident, there being only three and they were minor. During the attacks the number of casualties formed a

his duties as a part-time warden in Streatham and he is only one of many similarly placed, who show the same fine spirit of loyalty, often travelling long and awkward journeys to perform their spells of duty, when it would be so easy to apply for a transfer to the new and quieter district.

Owing to the lay-out of the streets, control of this K.100 incident could have been very awkward, but K.98, under D.P.W. Barker, immediately took over the damage in the Hillside Area, and kept I.O. Grose well posted with what was going on there. Doctors

Melvin and McGill were present, also Sister Rogers : Mrs. Perryman, Welfare Warden for K.100, did good work, so did Mr. Redpath, a chemist, of Norwood Road and Mrs. Skinner of the W.V.S.

BOMB After a short lull, the
22 next fly bomb crashed in the middle of the night on some shops and houses in Leigham Vale, demolishing several and wrecking many more. The K.96 wardens in this sector were at their action station only 80 yards from the bomb, and in consequence were all injured, or at least, severely shaken. Warden Underwood sustained a head injury, which subsequently necessitated four stitches, but, nevertheless, he ran a quarter of a mile to his post, where P.W. Gorringe was on duty, and before entering had the presence of mind to call out, " Don't be alarmed, but I'm bleeding a bit." After deli-

Photo : South Thames Press Agency.

" SHE'S ALIVE " : A trapped casualty has been reached at last and is given a drink through rubber tubing. Meanwhile the Heavy Rescue man in the foreground studies the problem of her release. (Bomb 14.)

27

vering his report, he was bandaged and laid on the floor until an ambulance could take him to hospital.

K.92 stepped into the breach excellently and S.W. Morley, of this post, acted as I.O., assisted by others, until D.P.W. Groves of K.96 arrived and took over, carrying on without a break for ten hours and discharging the responsibility very well.

Most of the casualties were recovered quickly and despatched to hospital or the First Aid Post, but the census cards and other information indicated there was likely to be a family of four sheltering in a reinforced room of one of the houses which looked just a mound of debris. By the lights of N.F.S. vehicles plus electric hand lamps the Rescue Parties under Station Officer Pavey set to work on this task. It proved a long and stubborn rescue, the rubble was so small that it had to be hand-picked away to avoid collapse on the trapped victims below.

At last contact was made, but another hour or two passed before the hole could be enlarged sufficiently to bring out the first casualty, a little girl of three or four. Dr. Russell had been standing by all the time and under his guidance the mother and girl had been given liquid through a rubber tube. Ever so carefully the Light Rescue men carried the stretcher with the little maid on it to a waiting ambulance. There, with the aid of a nurse, the doctor carried out a rapid examination, all the time chatting away to the child, giving reassuring answers to her questions about her brother " who went to school." Miraculously it seemed that she was almost unmarked and after another drink, which she insisted upon having through the rubber tubing again, she was rushed away to hospital for anti-shock treatment.

Meanwhile, the Rescue men found it impossible to extricate the mother, who was showing a marvellous spirit, until the other child had been removed from her side, and he was dead, although she did not know it. " We shall have to cover your face with a handkerchief to keep the dirt and plaster off while we shift this piece of wood," they lied, with infinite understanding and sympathy. Again the careful journey to the ambulance for the doctor's examination and for a few moments hope leapt up as a rumour flew round the incident that the boy's life was not extinct, but, alas, it was without foundation—Hitler had killed another innocent victim.

BOMB 23 A fly bomb on Streatham High Road in the middle of the afternoon on a spot near bus and tram queues sounds a nightmare for Civil Defence, but it happened and, amazing to relate, there was only one fatal casualty. The bomb appears to have struck a tree in the War Memorial Garden, then crashed on the pavement below, wrecking the police box

" SHE'S OUT—AND WE'VE JUST REACHED HIM " : The Incident Officer checks through his list of persons still missing with the L.C.C. Heavy Rescue Officer. Meanwhile, the Senior District Warden takes tea, and the C.D. Messenger returns from an important mission. (Bomb 16.)

and the wardens' post, also numerous shops which have since had to be pulled down. The Memorial itself was undamaged.

Fortunately it was early-closing day, and there were customers only in the hairdresser's. Mr. Ivor Jones, a chemist, was in the back of his smashed shop, but escaped unhurt. He immediately gave useful information *re* other shopkeepers and residents. By a miracle, too, there were no buses or trams passing at the precise moment, but the presence of mind of the driver of an approaching tram is to be highly commended, for he

braked hard as he saw the bomb dive and shouted to his passengers to duck, which they all did, thus avoiding injury. A R.E.M.E. captain in a passing car received an injury to his hand, but with a bandage from a warden wrapped round it, he drove on.

The S.D.W. arrived on the scene with Q.R.C.D. Letts and decided to act as I.O. himself as Post J.89 was out of action, Warden Webb being severely injured and his wife, also a warden, was a casualty too. Emergency communications were established via Divisional Office. D.P.W. Harrison of J.87 was another early arrival

29

and with **L.R.** Leader Chamberlain gave Webb first aid until an ambulance arrived. Light and Heavy Rescue parties turned out promptly, although both depots had been damaged and in a very short time operations were well in hand. Good work was done by cadets of the British Red Cross Society.

The police were requested to make a temporary traffic diversion, which they did, but in less than a quarter of an hour it was possible to dispense with this. Whilst the inevitable dislocation was at its height a military convoy went past and a lorry full of Americans pulled up and offered help—knowing that control was in train and adequate C.D. Services present, Harrison declined with thanks, assuring them that "everything is O.K." They looked round at the scene of devastation, shrugged their shoulders and saying, "Right-O-bud," continued on their way, doubtless musing on the queer ways of the British.

The difficulty of knowing how many people might have been passing and blown into the shops as they collapsed, meant the search had to be thorough and intensive— and it certainly was, but at last everybody was satisfied. After the last ambulance had been dismissed it was reported that yet another helpless casualty had been discovered in a wrecked licensed club. Upon further investigation, however, by no less a person than the Borough Controller himself, it was reported that the

Photo : South Thames Press Agency.

"A THEATRE WAS HIT ": Taken from the stage of Streatham Hill Theatre. Note the enormous hole torn in the wall of brickwork 27 inches thick. (Bomb 19).

casualty's condition was the result of opportunist stocktaking prior to abandoning the premises, rather than direct enemy action.

First Aid Post No. 6 at Streatham Baths had a busy afternoon, nearly 50 casualties being dealt with from this incident. The total during the fly bomb attacks was 305, and F.A.P. No. 5 had 270. Sister Rogers was in charge of both posts, whilst Doctors Hull and Stewart-Hunter were the respective medical officers. By efficient first aid and relieving the hospitals of congestion by minor cases, these posts contributed materially to the saving of lives, suffering and permanent injuries.

BOMB 24 Early next day, a fly bomb crashed in Southcroft Road at the junction of Salterford Road and made an unusually wide and deep crater. P.W. Greetham endeavoured to 'phone through the Express Report a minute later, but there was a hold-up, and a cyclist messenger had to be despatched. Mr. Waight, the I D.W., took charge as I.O. with Miss Windridge as clerk and both had a narrow escape when part of a damaged house collapsed around them.

This was to prove a fairly long and difficult incident, there being 46 casualties, including three fatal. D.P.W. Smith relieved Mr. Waight as I.O. in the later stages, and did very well. In some of the collapsed houses there was an element of doubt as to the number of persons present when the bomb fell, since it was the time when people would be setting out to work. Several enquiries were made by the police from employers, to resolve these queries. In one house the W.A.A.F. daughter was believed to be home, but the first hat to be found contained another name, which led to the discovery that the daughter's friend — also a W.A.A.F.—had stayed there overnight.

The tram-track was quickly cleared and the L.P.T.B. crane which arrived was not needed. Passengers on passing trams had a grand-stand view of the rescue operations, which were pushed forward very efficiently. The services included some from Mitcham, while wardens from Post G.59 (Tooting) gave welcome help during the day.

Characteristic of the spirit of fun shown by many in acute adversity was the man who ran out of his wrecked home, where he was endeavouring to salvage some of his belongings, crying, " Look what I've found ! Look what I've got ! " —holding up for all to see—an unbroken egg.

An extremely deaf lady had a marvellous escape, for she must have been within 15 feet of the bomb when it exploded. Later in the day, after treatment for head and wrist injuries, she was to be seen carrying tea to the rescue parties.

About noon the Chief Warden visited the incident and, after investigating the situation fully, expressed satisfaction with the progress made.

The operations of the afternoon became a search for a lad who had been delivering papers in Southcroft Road when the bomb fell. Commandant Wilson of the Light Rescue Service, knew the boy and gave valuable help, whilst wardens Grindrod and Mills traced out his calls from house to house and eventually located the exact spot, where search revealed first his bag of papers and then the boy himself, who must have been killed instantly.

The normal delivery of papers, milk and letters each day was a striking feature of the period — shopkeepers, too, remained open for '' business as usual,'' even if customers were fewer ; whilst the Locarno and local cinemas were always available to patrons, of whom there were no small number.

_____

That night Streatham was visited by the Parliamentary Secretary to the Ministry of Home Security. So tired that she was nearly out on her feet on arrival, Miss Wilkinson revived wonderfully over a cup of coffee and by a series of questions and pertinent comments, quickly proved her grasp of the situation. In company with the Senior District Warden and Major Sidenham Firth, J District Shelter Warden, she visited the large shelter near Streatham Station and the trenches on Streatham Common, both of which were full to capacity, but it was so late she did not speak to the shelterers, who were all asleep. Miss Wilkinson expressed herself as surprised and gratified to learn 55 per cent. of the Streatham wardens had qualified for four war - service chevrons — the maximum at that time.

Here, perhaps, is the point to pay a brief tribute to the shelter wardens of Streatham. Perhaps not so hazardous a job as most of Civil Defence, it is certainly an exacting one. Every night there are problems to be settled, differences between shelterers, missing and damaged equipment, registers to be checked and a dozen other minor duties. For the first time ever, Streatham shelters were full to capacity and that made it difficult to satisfy everybody. Through the constant nervous tension, people were generally rather '' edgy '' and the shelter wardens, with patience, tact and good humour, did a lot to maintain the high standard of morale with which the public using the shelters faced their ordeal.

Mr. Dineen in I District, Major Firth in J and Mr. Hack assisted by Mr. Robinson in K, all worked hard and did well ; whilst special mention must be made of the Deputy Divisional Shelter Officer (Miss McEwen) who provided efficient liaison with Headquarters, Wandsworth.

BOMB 25 Late one evening L.A.C. Marks was looking out of the window of Divisional Office (in which he worked for several

Photo : *South Thames Press Agency.*

NEXT MORNING : From the heap of debris on the left two live casualties were recovered and two dead. One of the wrecked shops was the wardens' action station. (Bomb 22.)

years) watching a military convoy move south, when a doodle-bug was heard approaching—it cut out, dived and exploded with a shattering roar and the inevitable cloud of dust and debris shot into the air, neatly framed by the window, which, strange to say, was still intact.

Dashing downstairs with the S.D.W., they jumped into a car, hooted their way across the stream of traffic and, quickly reached the scene of the incident at the junction of Oakdale and Grasmere Roads. Pulling out the folding table and chair which were always carried in the back of the car, and donning the I.O.'s blue hat cover, the S.D.W. took over, just as D.D.W. Tinson, who lives in the adjoining Valleyfield Road, fought his way through the still thick cloud of dust, to exclaim " Hullo, were you sitting there waiting for it ? "

The two sides of Oakdale Road are in different post areas, and the wardens of both J.89 and 91 rallied to the incident. The damage was extensive and the houses being large there was a lot of rescue work to be done.

Nurse Wing, a Ranyard District nurse, was quickly on the scene enquiring about one of her patients, and both then and later she gave valuable

Photo : South Thames Press Agency.

STREATHAM HIGH ROAD HIT : Taken only a few minutes afterwards, this picture shows the orderly search for casualties in the shops, and calm reaction of the public, police and tram staff. (Bomb 23.)

information. The occupants cards of both posts stood the test very well indeed.

All the occupants of No. 11 had marvellous escapes from injury, for No. 10 next door was demolished and all three occupants killed. As the explosion died away Mrs. Meldrum of the ground floor No. 11, went from under the stairs into the front room, and at that moment a piano fell through from the floor above and tore off one of her earrings as it passed, but left her otherwise unscathed. Two wonderful escapes in two minutes.

About 1 a.m. the Controller visited the incident with his assistant, Mr. Thurston. Both were a trifle dishevelled, having just '' made it '' when they dashed into an Anderson shelter to escape the blast of another fly bomb encountered during their tour of the borough.

The Rev. O. K. de Berry was about, collecting more '' bombed out '' persons for '' bed and breakfast'' at the Immanuel vicarage, and at one time he had no less than 19 staying there. Christianity in action.

All night long the search was continued under the efficient leadership of Station Officer Pavey of the L.C.C. Heavy Rescue Party Service. Persons were missing in four separate houses and consequently it was necessary to employ a large number of working parties. Commandant Wilson, in charge of the Streatham Light Rescue parties, was to be seen throughout this long incident —indeed, there were few of the 41 at which he was not quietly active.

Two cyclists were amongst the casualties and here again was a difficult problem of identity to be solved. Another query was whether a certain lady who had been away, staying with a daughter, had returned or not. Before this could be settled, it meant 'phone calls to the Admiralty and thence to Scotland. Sad to say, the lady had returned that very day, and lost her life.

P.W. Jones, of J.91, who had been acting as clerk, relieved the S.D.W. as I.O. and after a spell of seven hours or so, he, in turn, handed over to D.P.W. Ford of J.89 D. D. W. Tinson did splendid work throughout this incident. Similarly, Mr. Pavey handed over to Mr. Strudwick, and shortly after mid-day, the last casualty was recovered.

After another short interval of days, Sherwood Avenue, in Streatham Vale (Post J.84) was hit one afternoon. It was so near an earlier incident that for most of the property it was a second dose, but no easier to bear for all that. Casualties were fairly light—none fatal. Being day-time, the wardens came from various posts and

Photo : South Thames Press Agency.

"DOWNHEARTED? NOT ME!": Two Red Cross Cadets with a cheerful casualty they have just recovered and treated. (Bomb 23.)

D.P.W. Harrison of J.87 acted as I.O.

A woman and her son, whose house was smashed to bits, were saved from injury by the Anderson shelter to which they had run as the bomb approached. Shortly afterwards, when they were calmly discussing their narrow escape with a press photographer, the mother suddenly broke off and exclaimed with a little cry, " Oh, George, look ! our two lovely strawberry plants have gone from the top of the shelter," and it really seemed to distress her more at the moment than the loss of her home.

BOMB 27 The next fly bomb chose a beautiful summer's evening to dive into the middle of some allotments on Streatham Common. Casualties again were light, but the surrounding houses were badly blasted, including those of Alderman Carr and Doctor Caley, Borough Medical Officer of Health. Mrs. Caley is D.P.W., of J.91, the P.W. of which (Mr. P. Ormond-Jones) acted as I.O. The services were on the spot in record time and made a brave show, for instead of being spread, as usual, over several streets, they were parked in one long line. No less than 25 N.F.S. vehicles reported, and with all the other services there must have been a total of nearly fifty. S.W. Lawman was kept busy controlling this traffic, the bulk of which was quickly returned to depot.

One interesting and perhaps symbolical happening was that every growing thing on the allotments round the crater was cut off close to the ground (clean-shaven would best describe it) but a few weeks later the plants were throwing up fresh green growth. V.1 failed to quell the spirit of even British cabbages, they were determined to answer the call to " grow more food."

BOMB 28 Nearly a week later, the open space adjoining Covington Way was hit and although many houses were damaged, not a single casualty was recorded. D.P.W. Chaplin, of J.85, handled the incident, of which the most unusual feature was that the top of a large tree somehow caught fire.

BOMB 29 Post I.80 had the next bomb one morning before it was light, at the junction of Moyser Road and Furzedown Drive. The scene of devastation appeared particularly widespread, although, as it proved, casualties were not numerous. D.W. Waight acted as I.O. and was well served by the personnel of I.80 and the reinforcements from neighbouring posts.

The N.F.S., Rescue parties, Home Guard and Fire Guards all co-operated in the search for casualties, and rapid progress was made. A bulldozer helped to clear the roads of debris.

Mr. Morgan, the Fire Guard Staff Officer who had just been appointed Joint Deputy Controller with Mr. Thurston, put in an early appearance, as,

Photo : South Thames Press Agency.

A CASUALTY FOR F.A.P. 6 : A woman is helped along to the near-by First Aid Post. (Bomb 23.)

indeed, he did at all subsequent incidents.

Admiral Sir Edward Evans, one of London's Regional Commissioners, visited the incident, expressed satisfaction at the operations, sampled the Streatham mobile canteen's tea, signed the post log-book, took the address of a crippled ex-service man and left. The latter subsequently received £5 from a fund donated from South Africa, and the Admiral also sent a box of cigarettes to the wardens—a much-appreciated gesture.

The W.V.S. under Mrs. Irwin, the District Leader, did very good work and opened up the Inquiry Point in the wardens' stand-by post, where it operated for some time.

BOMB 30 The evening of the same day J.91 had its second bomb and this time it fell between Hopton and Valley Roads, directly opposite Hillhouse Road. Nearby wardens ran to the scene and S.W. Bookless was quickly hard at it, although the house he lived in was wrecked beyond repair.

P.W. Jones acted as I.O. for the third time, setting up his post on the corner of Hillhouse Road, but owing to the split nature of the incident, D.D.Ws. Sheppard and Tinson decided that a second point of control was necessary and installed D.P.W. Ford, of J.89, in Hopton Road.

Most of the casualties were recovered quickly and sent away for treatment, but one man proved very hard to find and the rescue parties toiled by the light of flares for many hours before his body was ultimately recovered. The night was a wet one and thoroughly unpleasant for all concerned.

It was with somewhat mixed feelings that P.W. Jones saw next day that the house beside which he had run his control post was labelled by the Surveyor "Dangerous Structure."

BOMB 31 Within twelve hours another fly bomb dropped in Post K.101, right on the borders of Lambeth. A laundry, a box factory and some cottages in Lutheran Place were all demolished, and much other damage. P.W. Pumphrett, of K.101, was the proprietor of the destroyed laundry and his manager was killed outright whilst keeping watch, his family being in the firm's shelter since they had been previously bombed out of their home. Notwithstanding this double loss, Mr. Pumphrett took on the job of I.O. and discharged the responsibility very commendably. The box factory belonged to the company of which Warden Wixcey is a director. The total casualties were about a dozen, including three fatal.

Nearby were the stables of the Co-op. milk distributing organisation, but the horses stood it very well, and there was little dislocation, thanks to quick action by the staff.

Twenty-three days after the incident a cat was recovered from one of the wrecked Lutheran Cottages and there can be little doubt it was incarcerated for the whole of this period, without serious ill-effects.

BOMB 32 Post J.89 received the next fly bomb and it fell in the very early hours, near the half-demolished St. Anselm's Church in the angle formed by Oakdale and Madeira Roads. D.P.W. Ford was I.O., with his control point in Madeira, and P.W. Frankford looked after the damage in Oakdale, while D.D.Ws. Sheppard and Tinson were early on the scene. Quickly Rescue Parties and N.F.S. set to work on the wrecked houses in both roads.

In Oakdale Road an Anderson shelter had been erected indoors in the hall—unfortunately it was not on a solid floor, there being a cellar underneath. Searchers eventually managed to get into the cellar from another point and the rescue work proceeded from above and below simultaneously, but to little avail, as it transpired the occupants had been killed outright.

Those who saw Mr. Faulkner's Welfare Play will remember the two charming elderly ladies, Mrs. Fawne snd Mrs. Dalton ; well, this house in Oakdale was the one to which Mr. Faulkner had taken the originals of these characters when they were bombed-out in an earlier raid, for it was the home of a niece who on this later occasion was killed. Incidentally, the two ladies again had to leave their home in Hopton Road and were evacuated first to Eardley Road Rest Centre and then to Leeds, but their staunch spirits remained unbroken despite this tragic double loss. This was one of several incidents at which Dr. Grosch was present.

In the later stages a small fire broke out in Oakdale Road and the many N.F.S. present appeared to compete for the honour of extinguishing it. During the operation quite a few people got rather wet.

BOMB There was a lull of a
33 few days then, just before midnight, the junction of Wavertree and Daysbrook Roads was hit, right opposite the Company H.Q. of the Home Guard and the Streatham High School for Girls, which both suffered severely. The incident was just in K.100, but K.99 post being nearer, they got there first, and P.W. Dando took charge as I.O. Some exceptionally fine

" GENTLY DOES IT " : A district nurse directs N.F.S. personnel lowering a woman casualty to a stretcher. The water bottle indicates a member of the Light Rescue Party. (Bomb 26.)

Photo : South Thames Press Agency

" WE WERE IN THERE " : This young man and his mother (wearing overall) dashed from the house on the right to the Anderson Shelter as fly bomb 26 approached, and so escaped injury. Pieces of the bomb are in the foreground. (Bomb 26.)

rescue work was performed here, including the recovery of two trapped casualties from a Morrison shelter on which a whole house had collapsed. One of the few letters of thanks received from rescued persons came from these ladies—here it is :—

> Warren Road Hospital,
> Guildford.

Dear Sir,

I should like to express my grateful thanks to the Civil Defence workers who rescued my friend and myself when the house was totally demolished by a direct hit. All the services seemed to arrive within a few minutes. Your marvellous and humane C.D. workers had found us under that mass of debris within an hour and by their skill and bravery had us out of that wonderful invention, the Morrison Table, in a few minutes. Would you convey to these men our very grateful thanks for saving our lives and to the doctors for their valuable services, so generously given after a long day's work.

I should also like to include the W.V.S., who so kindly prepared hot drinks for us and stood by, in spite of the great danger, during the night and welcomed us on our return from " the grave."

The ambulance driver and nurse soon had us at South London Hospital and I do thank them most sincerely for their help in face of great risk.

The hospital people were splendid and gave us great comfort and most kindly treatment till they sent us on here on 29th. I cannot sufficiently express my thanks and admiration for all who helped and for the splendid administration and co-operation of the Streatham Civil Defence. You are a marvellous body of men and women.

> Yours gratefully,
> H. C. A. Buysman,
> (40 years resident
> of Streatham).

An innovation at this incident was the loud-speaker kindly supplied by Tannoy Ltd., which D. P. W. Lean of

K.100 had fixed to the car of the S.D.W. earlier in the evening, saying " I hope we don't see you up in our area with it." It proved very useful in many ways.

Mr. Belham, K D.D.W., and the W.V.S. cared for the bombed-out in the school until coaches took them to the Rest Centre. The local Home Guard under Major Remnant were present in strength and helped a lot.

BOMB 34 Following this incident, K.92 was to have its third fly bomb, round about breakfast-time—as usual for them. Some big houses in Leigham Court Road were badly hit, but the bulk of the damage was on the other side of the road in the Borough of Lambeth. The Government-encouraged policy of evacuation proved its value at this incident, for although normally there were eleven persons living in the worst-damaged house, all had gone away but one, and he had spent the night with a neighbour. Useful confirmation of this happy situation was secured from the milk roundsman.

The casualties were three minor ones, and the incident was closed in a very short time. S.W. Morley again acted as I.O. in a satisfactory manner.

BOMB 35 Judged by the number of killed, the most serious of all Streatham's 41 fly bomb incidents occurred in Pendle Road (I.77) about three o'clock one morning, the death-roll numbering twelve. The bomb fell at the rear of the houses, bringing several down and involved some Anderson shelters from which a number of casualties were recovered. D.D.W. Ames acted as I.O. through the night, with Miss Enniss as clerk, handing over to his co-deputy Mr. Dineen, he being relieved in turn by D.P.W. Curtis, who held the fort all through the next day, during which rescue operations proceeded—the last body not being recovered until 5 p.m.

The loud-speaker on the S.D.W.'s car proved invaluable in securing information from the bystanders and neighbours, verifying the house census cards (which were carefully checked by Messrs. Walsh and Archer) and quickly resolving many of the rumours which inevitably float around any long incident. Mention should also be made of the two Randalls—C.D. messengers who gave splendid service for many hours.

This was a tragic incident for P.W. Woods, of Post I.78, for one of the fatal casualties was his sister-in-law.

It was one of the noisiest nights of the whole period, for a constant succession of flying bombs seemed to go over.

Another example of the marvellous spirit of the bombed-out occurred at the Streatham mobile canteen during the night, when an elderly lady in night attire and overcoat, with an eiderdown draped over her shoulders, came along for a cup of tea. As she drank it and munched a sandwich she said, "Dear me, if I'd known I was going to a tea-party I'd have put my best frock on." The laugh she got was very near to tears.

During the afternoon Lady Reading, chairman of the W.V.S., visited the Incident Inquiry Point, which was in charge of Mrs. Fisher, I.77 Post Leader. Mrs. Irwin, District Leader, and many others were also present. One task the W.V.S. undertook was to find a good home for a lovely pedigree Scotch terrier, which the bombed-out owners could not take with them to their evacuation address.

A novel feature was the assistance given to the Rescue parties by naval personnel who had been working in the area on first-aid repairs to damage caused by earlier bombs.

BOMB 36 As mentioned before, few part-time wardens were available in the area during business hours, and to deal with this position a mobile incident team for the whole Division was formed and stood-by adjacent to the N.F.S. headquarters. Column Officer Williams readily agreed to a request that this team should be transported in their vehicles, thus arriving within a few minutes of any bomb falling in Streatham during the day-time. Later, thanks to the courtesy of Streatham Hill Theatre, the team were loaned a van which was fitted up as a mobile incident control point.

Whilst the Pendle Road incident was still proceeding, another fly bomb fell in Post I.81, Abbottsleigh Road, and the mobile team went into action for the first time—it comprised D.P.W. Harrison as I.O., D.P.W. Rippon as clerk, White as loading ground warden and Moore as runner. The incident —a small one—was quickly and efficiently cleared. One must not forget to mention the warden of Post I.78, who proudly claimed he just managed to beat the mobile team to it.

BOMB 37 The third fly bomb in succession to fall in I District arrived before dawn, and chose the border of I.80, so that I.77 and I.81 were also affected. There was a large crater with burst gas and water mains in Moyser Road near the junction with Pretoria Road and property was damaged over a wide area.

D.D.W. Ames acted as I.O., with P.W. Archer, of I.81, as assistant : warden Alexander was clerk and warden Weston occupants checker. This job proved rather troublesome and over half an hour after the bomb fell there were 30 persons unaccounted for, although it seemed certain nothing like that number were still trapped. Once again the loud-speaker proved its worth, for within ten minutes of the announcement asking for all available information to be given to the I.O., the list of 30 missing had been reduced to two.

The Rescue services distinguished themselves, and made

another splendid recovery from a Morrison shelter in the heart of a wrecked house. There were two fatal casualties, and ten were taken to hospital. Permission to close the incident was granted within three hours of the bomb falling—quick work having regard to the circumstances. Wardens specially commended by the I.O. include Messrs. Greenhalgh, Harris, Hartland, Habberfield, Raybaud, Miss Hill and Miss Murray. The two messengers Randall, also Letchford, were particularly useful.

Whilst the rescue operations were proceeding, the Streatham mobile canteen served tea and sandwiches to C.D. personnel and the bombed-out — as, indeed, it did at nearly every incident.

The Borough Controller visited the incident and laid emphasis on the need for full after-raid services. It was, therefore, sheer cussedness that the Ministry of Food canteen ordered to supply breakfast to the bombed-out reported to Moyser Road, *Wanstead*, instead of *Wandsworth*. Later in the day canteens and other facilities were made available and much appreciated. Mrs. Nut-

ting, the Borough Organiser of the W.V.S., took a special interest in this after-raid help.

In Pretoria Road, which was badly knocked about, one householder was carefully sweeping the broken tiles and glass from his gateway, although it looked as if the whole house might collapse any moment. " What gets me wild,'' he confided to a passing warden, '' is that I've just paid my ruddy rates in advance ! ''

Photo : South Thames Press Agency.

" YOU'LL BE ALL RIGHT " : A smiling Ambulance Driver takes over a minor casualty from a lady warden, watched by Mr. David Robertson, M.P. for Streatham. (Bomb 26).

MORE BLAST DAMAGE : The Streatham High School for Girls was badly damaged one night. The photo was taken early next day. (Bomb 33.)

BOMB 38 I District's run of ill-luck continued, and next day Aldrington Road, Streatham Park, was hit at the junction with Ullathorne Road. P.W. Archer, of I.81, took over as I.O., with Senior Fire Guard Watkins as clerk. The only casualty was a passer-by, who was quickly despatched to hospital. There was a large gas main alight and a big tree had been almost uprooted—both these dangers were dealt with by the ever-resourceful N.F.S. Military personnel placed at the disposal of the I.O. were used to control traffic and the Fire Guard Sector Captain gave very useful information for the check-up of occupants in the damaged houses. The total time of this incident from bomb-fall to official closure was just forty minutes —surely a record for speed.

BOMB 39 K.99 next received a fly bomb at a pre-breakfast hour. It fell in Tierney Road, near Streatham Place, bringing down five big houses and damaging a large amount of surrounding property. Casualties occurred in Montrell, Sulina and Christchurch Roads, in addition to the two mentioned. About 8 went to hospital and 20 to F.A.P.5.

Streatham Place is on the narrow side, but it proved possible to operate this incident and yet permit normal traffic, including buses, to use the road. This was due to close co-operation between the police and C.D. Services. The troops of a military convoy which

44

went by seemed to be extremely interested in the damage caused.

P.W. Dando was I.O., being well supported by the wardens of K.99 and neighbouring posts.

Towards the close of the incident a fire broke out in the wreckage of one house, probably due to an electrical short. The N.F.S. were recalled and quickly dealt with this.

BOMB 40 Fly bombs Nos. 40 and 41 fell within fifteen minutes of each other, early one Sunday morning. The earlier gave K.97 its fifth, which thus achieved the unenviable highest record for any Streatham Post.

The bomb fell between houses in Bellasis and Thornton Avenues, and caused much damage in both these and other nearby roads.

Warden Steele again acted as I.O. in a very satisfactory manner. D.P.W. Hansen was injured by debris from the explosion, but persisted in carrying on. At one stage he was persuaded to get into an ambulance, but before it moved off

Photo: Streatham News

" THE NAVY'S HERE " :   The mobile canteen serves tea to naval ratings helping with first-aid repairs to properties in Pendle Road area. W.V.S. from the nearby Incident Inquiry Point are also refreshed.   (Bomb 35.)

he was out again and quite late in the afternoon was still about the scene of the accident, with a bandage round his head.

Fifteen casualties were sent to hospital and rather less to First Aid Post No. 5. Fortunately, there were no fatal casualties. During the day the Mayor of Wandsworth (Alderman Bonney) visited this incident and No. 41 in I District, accompanied by the Chief Warden (Alderman Evan Rees). He talked with many of those whose homes had been damaged, and congratulated the wardens on doing a good job.

BOMB 41 The last fly bomb to be recorded in this story fell on I.79 at the junction of Crowborough and Ramsdale Roads, great damage being done in Gorse Rise and other roads in the neighbourhood. This was a remarkable incident in that there were no trapped casualties at all, nor were there any fatalities. The bomb fell on the rear gardens in the midst of a cluster of Anderson shelters, and the degree of protection afforded was amazing. It was undoubtedly due to this, plus the amount of evacuation which had taken place, that the number of casualties was so low.

P.W. Greetham, although on the sick list, took charge of the incident at the start, and when D.D.W. Ames took over, carried on very pluckily as his assistant. For once, it was a lovely sunny morning and whether this had anything to do with it or not, the standard of public morale was really exceptional. Being Sunday, nearly everybody was at home and the thirsty work of clearing up brought a constant stream to the Streatham C.D. Mobile Canteen. Three times were supplies replenished and the staff were " flat out " for nearly four hours.

The W.V.S. opened an I.I.P. in the pavilion of Furzedown, which was the nearest suitable place available.

A considerable number of Tooting Home Guards worked both in the morning and afternoon helping to tidy up houses, move furniture and deal with first-aid repairs. In the latter connection supplies of materials were immediately made available at I.80 warden's stand-by post—the issue being announced over the loudspeaker. A Salvation Army Canteen supplying soup at mid-day was similarly made known. Furniture removals and first aid repairs also went forward under borough auspices, getting into action with commendable speed. At a later stage both the mobile baths and laundry attended.

Sir Ernest Gowers, Senior Regional Commissioner, visited the scene during the morning, having just come from another borough in which there had been an incident with very heavy casualties. Discussing this with the S.D.W., the latter said, " Well, in that respect we've been lucky," and Sir Ernest replied, " I certainly never expected to hear anybody in Wandsworth say they have been lucky with fly bombs ! '' But when one thinks of crowded shopping centres, railway platforms in the rush hours, churches, places of amusement, bus and tram queues, public houses, restaurants and the many other places where people congregate, indeed one can say that, from the casualty angle, things in Streatham might have been worse.

THE BALANCE SHEET.

How shall we sum up this two months' ordeal ? It was a period of almost constant danger, of never knowing who was '' for it '' next, and under the strain reserves broke down, producing a feeling of universal comradeship and desire to help each other, which in turn created a strange exaltation, a sort of common pride in sticking it out.

On the debit side we have the following official figures for the Streatham Division alone :—

CASUALTIES

Killed	....	84
Seriously injured	....	335
Slightly injured		567
		986

DAMAGE TO PROPERTIES

Demolished, or damaged beyond repair	860
Heavily damaged	4,755
Less seriously damaged	11,512
	17,127

This equals 88 per cent. of total number of houses in Streatham.

What is there to set on the credit side ? No official figures admittedly ; but surely a major factor in the successful invasion of France by the liberating armies was the command of the air by the R.A.F. That this command was almost undisputed by the Luftwaffe, must have been largely due to the diversion of the German aircraft industry for many months from fighter planes to flying bombs.

Hence it may well be, that the ordeal of Southern England, of which Streatham was a heavily engaged area, contributed substantially to the success of the invasion and especially to the avoidance of thousands of casualties by aerial attack during the landings. If this is so, then undoubtedly there is a credit balance, notwithstanding the tragic total of loss and suffering represented by the debit side.

PHOTOGRAPHS : *All fees and costs have been generously waived by the owners of the copyright photographs reproduced in this book, in order to assist the Streatham Comforts Fund and their co-operation is most gratefully acknowledged.*

Those marked " South Thames Press Agency '' were taken by Mr. Denis R. Thiel, the Editor and Proprietor of the Agency (also of South Thames Studios), 70, Streatham High Road, S.W.16. As an M.O.I. accredited photographer, Mr. Thiel was often at the incident within a few minutes of the fly-bomb falling—hence the dramatic action pictures he was able to secure.

THE METROPOLITAN BOROUGH OF WANDSWORTH.

Mayor and Chairman of Civil Defence Control Committee :
ALDERMAN WM. C. BONNEY, J.P., L.C.C.

Town Clerk and A.R.P. Controller :
MAJOR R. H. JERMAN, M.A., M.C., O.B.E.
Deputy Controllers : L. MORGAN and H. G. THURSTON.
Officer-in-Charge of Control Room : P. BURR.
Officers-in-Charge of Sub-Control : W. EBLING, and G. HERBERT.

Chief Warden :	*Casualty*	*L.C.C. Heavy*	*W.V.S.*
ALDERMAN EVAN REES.	*Services :*	*Rescue Service.*	*Borough*
Deputy :	DR.F.G.CALEY.	*District*	*Organiser :*
ALDERMAN F. JORDAN	*Light Rescue*	*Rescue Officer:*	MRS. M.
(later) H. W. FRAY.	*Service :*	F. BUTCHER.	NUTTING.
Shelter Staff Officer :	*Commandant*	*Deputy:*	
D. J. FITZ-SIMONS.	J. B. HORTON.	S. WILSON.	
Fire Guard Staff Officer :			
D. CHURCH.			

STREATHAM DIVISION.

The names of some of those who held office in the various Streatham services during the fly bomb attacks are recorded here, but it should be realised that limitations of space alone, not lesser degree of merit, rules out the naming of the entire personnel. Moreover, it would be the special wish of those mentioned, that tribute should be paid to their predecessors who laid the foundations of Streatham's Civil Defence so well and truly.

DIVISIONAL OFFICE.

KENNETH BRYANT, W. H. HEAD, MISS J. C. MCEWEN, A. V. HORRELL,
G. T. MEEKINGS, MISS J. J. SMITH.
C.D. Messengers (Red Cross Cadets) J. BULL, B. COLLINS, H. JARMAN.

WARDEN SERVICE.

DISTRICT WARDENS.

Senior District Warden—KENNETH BRYANT.

" I " District—T. H. WAIGHT.	*Deputies*—W. J. AMES, W. J. DINEEN.
" J " District—W. J. HAGGER.	„ A. SHEPPARD, E. J. TINSON.
" K " District—E. W. GARRETT.	„ T. J. BRYANT, C. T. HACK.

48

POST WARDENS AND DEPUTIES.

Post I.77 —P. Walsh, W. C. Curtis (I.O.), F. A. Randall.
" I.78 —A. J. A. Woods (I.O.), E. H. Long, W. A. H. Usher.
" I.79 —F. G. Greetham (I.O.), F. J. Child, H. J. Miller.
" I.80 —R. J. Goldsworthy (I.O.), F. H. Matthews (I.O.), H. F. Stanford.
" I.81 —F. G. Archer (I.O.), A. H. Rippon, L. Watts (I.O.).
" J.82 —W. C. Ratcliffe-Franklin, F. C. Loweth, E. R. Thomas (I.O.).
" J.83 —F. A. Joslin, R. C. Cook, G. Murrell.
" J.84 —W. Thompson, F. C. B. Dalton, G. S. Theedam.
" J,85 —E. G. Edwards, E. J. Brind (I.O.), S. E. Chaplin (I.O.).
" J.86 —G. F. Byers, J. S. Bell (I.O.), E. G. Osborn.
" J.87 —P. H. Harrison, C. W. Harrison (I.O.), M. Westfield.
" J.88 —N. Narracott, W. J. Kingcome (I.O.), J. S. Rogers.
" J.89 —T. A. Frankford (I.O.), A. M. Bates, C. C. Ford (I.O.).
" J.90 —W. P. Emuss (I.O.), C. S. Cox, B. W. Oakley.
" J.91 —P. Ormond-Jones (I.O.), Mrs. Caley, G. Robertson.
" K.92 —A. Brimicombe, W. B. Ashwell, P. M. Chapman.
" K.93 —P. Savoie, J. Gibb, F. H. Scammell.
" K.94 —C. O. Randall (I.O.), Mrs. Horsey, W. Rosam (I.O.).
" K.95 —S. L. Hawes, A. Lister-Kaye (I.O.), W. R. Waight (I.O.).
" K.96 —C. M. Gorringe (I.O.), H. M. Groves (I.O.), H. J. Henderson (I.O.).
" K.97 —E. G. Lumley, J. Hansen, A. H. Neale (I.O.).
" K.98 —J. G. Sumner, H. Barker, J. K. Wilkie (I.O.).
" K.99 —H. E. Dando (I.O.), H. J. Collett, S. Snipper.
" K.100—R. Fraser (I.O.), H. J. Grose, F. G. Lean (I.O.).
" K.101—D. G. Pumfrett (I.O.), P. T. Bedser (I.O.), A. R. Holmes.

QUALIFIED INCIDENT OFFICERS—WARDENS.

(Excluding those previously mentioned.)

H. Abrahams, R. N. Brade, N. Cartlidge, W. C. Foord, H. E. Hill, J. H. Horton, J. S. Ingram, F. J. Jones, F. H. Keightley, G. H. Knight, F. H. Lawman, G. W. Leach, S. G. Letts, W. J. Morley, F. E. Pyne, C. Read, P. H. Smith, H. E. Steele, E. E. Vauzelles, G. C. Watt, W. L. Webb, J. H. Whitfield.

Q.R.C.D.—WARDENS.

N. Cartlidge, C. C. Ford, J. Hansen, S. G. Letts and T. A. Taylor.

SHELTER WARDENS.

" I " —District Shelter Warden—W. J. Dineen.
　　　　Post Shelter Wardens —W. C. Curtis, W. G. Searle, A. Kelvie, E. Harris.

" J " —District Shelter Warden—Major Sidenham Firth.
　　　　Post Shelter Wardens —J. W. Ayers, R. Tonkin, W. C. Moore, R. Thiel, Mrs. Curtis, A. Thompson, Miss V. B. Skeen, A. Plant, Mrs. Smithers.

" K "—District Shelter Warden—C. T. Hack. Deputy—A. Robinson
　　　　Post Shelter Wardens —W. A. Gray, N. J. Bidlake, T. Gratwick, F. W. West, H. Wright, Miss J. Cave, C. A. Sully.

STREATHAM'S RAID WELFARE SCHEME.

Divisional Welfare Officer—CANON D. M. SALMON.

" I " —District Welfare Warden—MISS MILNES.
    Post Welfare Wardens —MRS. LARKIN, MRS. CAPEL, MRS. FARRANTS, MRS. HOWELLS, MISS AMOR.

" J " —District Welfare Warden –H. L. FAULKNER.
    Post Welfare Wardens —A. E. VOSE, MRS. SMITH, J. LAWRENCE, MRS. EDWARDS, MRS. OSBORN (*Deputy District*), MRS. JARVIS, MISS L. NARRACOTT, J. J. F. JOHNSON, A. PLANT, MRS. SMITH.

" K "—District Welfare Warden—E. BELHAM.
    Post Welfare Wardens —C. H. MASTERS, MRS. CROSSKEY, MRS. RAMSDEN, MRS. BINGHAM, MRS. TRENERRY, M. W. HUNT (*Deputy District*), MRS. BARKER, MISS E. WELLS, MRS. PERRYMAN, A. LOCKWOOD.

Also District and Post Leaders of the W.V.S.

L.C.C. HEAVY RESCUE SERVICE.

Station Rescue Officers —D. J. PAVEY and G. A. STRUDWICK.
Station Rescue Foremen—G. ELLIOTT and G. REGAN.
Party Leaders   —E. CHEALL, A. CLARK, G. PARKINSON, H. BRANSGROVE, E. STEEL, S. SALTER, J. McFARLANE, F. STAPLETON.

LIGHT RESCUE SERVICE.

Officer-in-charge —A. W. WILSON.
Station Officers —E. BARNARD and G. RUSSELL-OWEN.
Sergeants   —E. H. BISH, H. W. BROWN, P. H. G. MATTHEWS, L. S. VINEY, R. G. PARKER, D. C. WEST, J. W. JELLY, A. E. CHAMBERLAIN.
Corporals   —H. W. BALL, H. W. BIRD, A. L. CHAMBERLAIN, J. F. HENNESSY, L. C. QUINN, A. C. STANLEY, W. F. BOUTER, A. T. FUGGLE, E. HALL, J. C. HICKEN, W. A. HAND, G. H. OVERALL, F. W. WESTON, G. H. WINTER.

NATIONAL FIRE SERVICE.

N.F.S. Officers who attended fly bomb incidents in Streatham include:
Divisional Officers—BAKER and DENYER.
Column Officers —ANDREWS and WILLIAMS.
Company Officers —ANNISON, BOXALL, LANGFORD, SHARR and SKINNER.
Section Leaders —BLATCHFORD, COLBOURN, DIBBS, DUNK, EVEREST, FITZGERALD, FRENCH, GUY, HARRIS, LOGAN, SCALES, SPICER, STURGES, WARD and WATERS.

FIRE GUARD

Divisional Fire Guard —COUNCILLOR F. H. CAMPBELL, H. E. WATES (Training Officer), W. H. CHANTLER, MRS. D. M. CHUBB, MRS. L. G. DAVENPORT, A. JACKSON, MRS. M. R. ROSS, J. W. THURSBY, J. VALLES, H. V. WALKER.

" I " —Head Fire Guard —C. TURNER.
      Senior Fire Guards—J. M. IRWIN, G. TRODD, E. F. SAINSBURY,
                    S. C. LAWRENCE, T. WALKINS.

" J " —Head Fire Guard —S. A. COTTON.
      —Senior Fire Guards—C. H. BURCHETT, M. TORCH, W. W. CHARMAN,
                    C. A. WAKELING, J. B. NOEL, H. CARTER,
                    T. A. WALSH, A. E. HENDERSON, H. S.
                    DOVE, H. K. TAYLOR.

" K "—Head Fire Guard —H. L. HUGHES.
      —Senior Fire Guards—K. M. CURRIE, B. J. LYNES, A. E. SMART,
                    W. C. WYATT, S. LEVY, R. H. EGLETON,
                    E. G. ALLARD, A. L. MIDDLETON,
                    S. C. COLMAN.

FIRST AID POSTS Nos. 5 and 6.

Sister-in-charge—MRS. D. ROGERS.

Deputy—No. 5—	Deputy—No. 6—
MISS M. E. LANGLEY.	MISS D. BARKER.
Medical Officer—	Medical Officer—
DR. STEWART-HUNTER.	DR. G. R. HULL.

WOMEN'S VOLUNTARY SERVICES.

Sub-Centre Organiser—MRS. CRISP (until injured), then MRS. KNIGHT.

MRS. CRONK, MRS. LARLHAM, MRS. SILKSTONE, MRS. THORNLEY and
                MISS V. WRIGHT.

" I " District Leader —MRS. IRWIN.
      Post Leaders   —MRS. GENTLEMAN, MRS. THURGOOD, MRS.
                    MANLEY, MRS. FISHER, MRS. ETCHES.

" J " District Leader —MRS. BAILEY.
      Post Leaders   —MRS. LODGE, MRS. CLARKE, MRS. THOMPSON, MRS.
                    RANDALL, MRS. JARVIS, MRS. FROST, MRS.
                    DARE, MRS. LINDENBOOM, MISS KIDBY,
                    MISS MAYNARD.

" K " District Leaders —MRS. KINNERSLEY and MRS. SKINNER.
      Post Leaders   —MRS. HORRELL, MRS. SAVOIE, MRS. O'DWYER,
                    MRS. McDERMOTT, MRS. WEBB, MRS. LEVY,
                    MRS. MORGAN, MRS. CASS, MRS. WARNER,
                    MRS. GOODRIDGE.

Amongst the many others who helped, great assistance was received from :—

      London Auxiliary Ambulance Service.
      Borough Engineer's Department.
      The Police (Streatham and Tooting Divisions).
      The Home Guard (30th and 31st London).
      Mobile Canteens, Baths and Laundry.
      L.C.C. Rest Centres.
      London Telephone Service.
      Gas, Electricity and Water undertakings.

CPSIA information can be obtained
at www.ICGtesting.com
Printed in the USA
BVHW042332310521
608489BV00016B/3018